*Snap Sh*

# VOYAGE TO ST. KILDA

## By

## Monica Weller

First published in the United Kingdom in 1998

by Monica Weller

ISBN No. 1 873597 05 3

Trade Distribution:
Clan Book Sales Ltd.,
The Cross,
Doune, Perthshire. FK16 6BE

printed by
Adlard Print & Reprographics
The Old School, The Green, Ruddington, Notts NG11 6HH

# INTRODUCTION

Inspiration for this book has come from my friends on the Isle of Harris in the Outer Hebrides. Uncomplicated people whose lives are punctuated by love, friendship and tradition. Ina and Angus Morrison have shown me great compassion each year when I could not get to St. Kilda. In 1997, my joy was their joy when I returned from the 'islands on the edge'. My story is dedicated to my family who I know will understand the emotion I felt whilst writing and photographing "Voyage to St. Kilda".

Monica Weller

Robert Stevenson, skipper, from Tarbert, Isle of Harris.

# Voyage to St. Kilda

FIRST DAY

Eleven of us assembled at Leachin on the outskirts of Tarbert, Isle of Harris. West Loch Tarbert was bathed in sunshine. A picture of tranquillity. The water gently lapping against the stone steps of the tiny pier. It would probably be the best day of the year. A day when the sea and land would be enveloped in a warm glow. The most perfect conditions for our voyage to St. Kilda.

Chrisalda Morrison had thrown open the dining room window on Sunday night and asked me if I was going to St. Kilda on Monday. I immediately replied "I'm going if you're going." A phone call would be made and we would take the last two places on the boat. Eleven passengers in total would attempt to make the risky journey to Hirta, Boreray and the Stacs Armin and Lee.

My story begins on Monday 18th August 1997. At 11 a.m we set off in the 58 foot cruise boat skippered by Robert Stevenson. We were instructed about safety skills in the event of any emergencies at sea. The voyage to St. Kilda, 50 miles west of Harris is dangerous. It is no ordinary day trip. I have waited six years for the conditions to be right. Today, at last, everything was perfect.

We passed Hillcrest, where we stay with Chrisalda's parents, Angus and Ina Morrison. We waved frantically as if our journey would take us away for months. Struan, the sheep dog, was tearing up and down the front path of the croft, obviously delighted with the feelings of anticipation.

The Isle of Harris has its own magnetic charm. It is what draws us back each year. The rare peace and naturalness of lifestyle is almost impossible to describe in words.

Chrisalda

Each year, during our visits, when I have had time to contemplate the very meaning of life, my desire to travel to St. Kilda has got stronger and stronger. A place which I believe is peace on earth. A place to feel completely at one with the very essence of life itself. To me it is not just the amazing people I have read about, who battled against all odds to survive. Nor is it the immense wild life uninterrupted in their natural surroundings. Nor is it the abandoned village on Hirta we have seen pictures of. To me, I hope it will be a few hours when mind and body come together to witness the miracles of all the earth's natural forces. To be enlightened and uplifted in spirit. The tremendous power of huge grey rocks rising from the sea and the wildness of a land unchanged since creation itself. These are the reasons I want to experience a voyage to St. Kilda.

My fellow companions were all very different but with one burning ambition. To share the experience of sailing 50 miles out into the Atlantic and witness with their own eyes, a unique place of such history and raw beauty.

During the first three hours some of the passengers felt very bad. Their equilibrium sadly departed at the quayside in West Loch Tarbert. The sickness showed in their faces. Roddy, a retired Cal Mac Skipper nursed his wife at the front of the boat as her body became more intolerant of the gliding action of the boat. Although the sea seemed calm, the waves were long and the troughs were more pronounced. One by one the voyagers succumbed to pills and potions in an attempt to correct the desperate feelings of sickness.

Lunch was served at about 2 p.m. Sandy, the cook had prepared a banquet. From the 4 foot square galley kitchen, a memorable meal was presented. Nearly all of us ate well. Then to my horror, after I had attempted to make a pot of tea in the hot wobbling galley, my eyes started to roll. My face went green. I felt hot, then cold, then hot again. The tea was abandoned as I flung myself up the stairs onto the deck. I refused to be sick. I devoured a sea sick pill and within half an hour I felt tired and lay down on a pile of all weather clothing and cam-corders strewn about the seats on deck. I slept. No more than ten minutes. But it was a deep sleep. Suddenly I heard someone shout Wales. I was nudged as they shouted at me again. Wales. I sat bolt upright, confused. Where was I? Was I in Wales? Or was I in Scotland? I had no idea where I was. Then I realised, whoever was shouting, was referring to mammals – whales. They knew I was recording the trip with my camera and the sighting of a whale was an occurrence I should not miss. But I did. The excitement of forgetting where I was, ended my feelings of sickness. That was all in the past. I had found my sea legs. They had obviously just been in hiding. I was ready to face anything.

Fourteen miles out from Harris, St. Kilda came into view. There was great excitement. On the horizon, bathed in a fine mist, the purple shapes of the group of islands appeared as if by magic. We knew we were going to make it. There was no turning back. I nodded off to sleep again. I think I had a smile on my face. When I regained consciousness we were fourteen miles away from St. Kilda.

Boreray, with Stac Lee (left of picture) and Stac An Armin (right of picture).

Sailing in a south west direction towards Village Bay,
Conachair 430m rising above the cloud.

Chrisalda and I stood huddled together at the back of the boat watching the islands come closer and closer. This was truly amazing. The gannets which we had seen in small numbers earlier, were gathering momentum. They were gracefully skirting the boat. Then in formations of six or seven, in red arrows fashion, they skimmed the surface of the water as if to form a welcoming party. There was no aggressive diving or flocking. Just grace and smoothness of action, guiding us closer to St. Kilda. Their piercing eyes and ivory and amber plumage were fully visible as they showed off their territory proudly. Puffins bobbing up and down in the water, took off in their customary manner. Flapping their wings madly as if just learning to fly. Then releasing their legs and skidding across the surface of the water, with their brakes on! They are such quaint little characters. Almost like clowns of the sea.

## THE ARRIVAL

We steamed directly to Village Bay on Hirta. It was a grand vision. The semi circular bay. The hundreds of bee hive like cleits cluttering the hillside behind the clear remains of the village street. The strange skinny brown sheep dotted around the scene. The thousands of sea birds forming a skin over the protective cliffs either side of the bay. A scene virtually indescribable. But the faces of the intrepid travellers and the crew told the whole story. A seven hour sea trip had focused our thoughts. The excitement and fear. The sickness. The detailed discussions and expectations. All the emotions, so obviously different from each member of our party, had been smoothed into one of unified awe and amazement. Moments of silence. Eyes close to tears. Smiles of satisfaction.

The dinghy was positioned beside the boat. Chrisalda, Sarah, Jonathan and myself formed the first landing party. Climbing out onto the concrete steps of the pier was a very special event. Chrisalda knelt down and kissed the ground. We had actually made it. The feeling was so marvellous as we made our way to the white painted Factor's House.

Everyone landing on St. Kilda must register with the Warden from the National Trust for Scotland and Scottish Natural Heritage, who instructs the visitors about conduct on the island. There are no laws, but this island is such a special place, and the natural wildness must be respected. We spoke briefly but it was no normal conversation. I was rendered virtually speechless by the emotional arrival. The warden was obviously not interested in discussing his six month 'shift' on the remotest outpost in the British Isles, but he did reel off the number of TV programmes he had appeared in, both in the UK and as far away as Japan and America. Mentioned on Radio 4 recently, he is clearly a man in demand, to tell his story about the abandoned island. About the working parties and the involvement with the army, whose presence is quite obvious with its' grey military buildings on the shore of Village Bay.

I felt privileged to walk down the village street. The neat cottages to our right and the remains of the cultivated land to our left, leading down to the shore. It was not pure nostalgia which lead me to St. Kilda. My thoughts, as I picked my way down the remains of granite stone paving, turned to questioning the meaning of life itself. In a place of such history, where time literally has stood still, my mind darting from questions of evolution, to human behaviour, of power struggles and to survival of our species. St. Kilda's history cut off in its prime and even now, dramatic changes are due to happen again with the army's imminent withdrawal of soldiers from the island. Chrisalda and I signed the visitor's book in the museum. The feeling that St. Kilda would become a shrine in future years concerned me. Towards the end of the street the cottages were more derelict, some of them no more than piles of stones. It was a poignant moment, as the further we walked, the more the houses were literally disappearing under our eyes.

Last light on the village street, Hirta.

The Factor's House

I walked in solitude onto the fields which would once have been cultivated. A few skinny soay sheep trotted past with their goat like movements. Strange animals, wild and scrawny. They have survived the traumatic times and they fill in the jigsaw between past and present.

The sun was rapidly going down over hundreds of cleits on the hillside. The horseshoe bay would soon be in darkest shadow as I made my way back to the dinghy to return to the boat for supper.

A huge full moon positioned itself next to Boreray.

We were ferried back to the pier after another memorable meal, to visit the Puff Inn, a modern pub within the army complex. We paid our £1 each to join the Club, entitling us to drink in the bar.

By 2 a.m. the last of our party had been safely transferred back to the boat where we would spend the night.

# MOONLIGHT

Silver dreams, silver lights
Jewels of the night.
The bleakest thoughts polished
By the iridescent might
Of moonshine, moonlight.

Beacon in the darkest sound
Transpose the dulled and tired mind
To shining status once again
The saviour, solid will remain
As lunar spells the sterling hour
To dusk when we regain our power.

The night when man does pray
For earthly riches him endow
Strange thoughts, nightmares somehow
Reality turns to fantasy and dreams.
In truth our precious lives 'tween
Night and day are punctuated by
The silver charms of doubt and fear.

Solid, simple lunar light
More precious than a bulb which dies
Tarnish merely foils your glow
As clouds move slowly 'cross your face.
Once more the trophy of the night
Gleams brightly showing us a sight.
Lion hearted, soft and brave
A hallmark, there to show the way.

Sarah

A sombre reminder of the missile tracking station on St. Kilda.

SECOND DAY

By 8 a.m. it was clear that the weather conditions were deteriorating. Village Bay looked angry. The previous day's calm waters had disappeared during the night. Our trip ashore was cancelled. The mood on board the boat changed as Robert the skipper, informed us of probable bad weather conditions coming up. Force 5/7 was a possibility. He was not prepared to risk our lives in dangerous seas and decided to leave Village Bay immediately after breakfast. We would go straight to the stacs and then head for home.

The largest sea cliffs in U.K. with Mina Stac to the right.

Our cruise boat crashed into the choppy sea, outside the protection of the horseshoe bay. Within a quarter of an hour the most wondrous sight came into view. The formidable shapes of Boreray, Stac Armin and Stac Lee were looming in front of us. All the pictures ever printed or painted cannot express the tremendous feeling of power, created by the huge monoliths rising from the sea.

I felt overwhelmingly small next to these greatest creations on earth. The dome shape of Boreray, black, hard and glistening, and white, where it is coated with sea birds. Extreme opposites of colour and strength. The ancient rocks combined with the teaming wild life created sights too great to put into words.

Glancing around the boat my companions were mesmerised by the scene. Speechless and staring, as the immenseness of the stac overpowered them. Then, as we approached Stac Armin and Stac Lee, I felt wave upon wave of being surrounded by the very beginning of life, where all earth's forces come together. Of lightness and darkness. Of mist and brightness creating a force so huge. The very beginning of life and the end together as one. A place of raw beauty, a kingdom of its own.

Approaching Stac Lee

Stac Lee to the left and Boreray to the right of picture.

Sea stac, south side of Boreray.

# FROM DARKNESS TO LIGHT

The road winds with
Broken tracks and paths
Where rocks are strewn
To stumble and fall.
In darkness, the treachery
Of life's byways
Hidden uncertain lanes
Self doubt and fear.

Then light with all its power
Breaks through the depths
Creating pools of faith
Mankind is guided
Honesty, truth and love
The route is clear.

With search lights from the sun
Most awesome striking rays
A danced performance, picture show
Projects the plains and heights
Unbounded, totally free
The choice defined
Uncluttered pathways, bold
With subtle hues

All complex shadows, pushed aside
The dawning of awareness
Lights the way.

Like a shark rising up from the sea, Stac Lee.

North East point of Boreray.

'A place of raw beauty, a Kingdom of its own'.

From left to right - Boreray, Hirta shrouded by cloud, Stac Lee and Stac An Armin

Sea Cliffs on the East side of Boreray.

The gannets formed a solid canopy above our heads. They were close to us and far away. There was no intimidation. The birds formed plains of light against the darkness of the black pointed giants rising from the sea. The scene was like a theatre where stage sets can be altered to suit a mood. But this scene included every different set imaginable, and the performance still retaining perfect symmetry. It was quite clear, looking at the intrepid travellers that we were all sharing the same experience. A power of greatness in this wild place and a sense of our own insignificance on this earth. There were moments of complete clarity of thought when the mind was cleansed and the way forward was clear. Then a mist covered the dense volcanic rock, forming yet more tones of grey and the perspectives changed again creating a greater closeness of the rocks, then, in an instant, it was changed. Clouded, as in life.

The experience of witnessing the tremendous monoliths of Boreray, Stac Armin and Stac Lee was, for me, like seeing the whole of life before my eyes. Where opposites worked in perfect harmony.

East face of Boreray.

The magnificent Stac Lee.

It was over. The Stacs disappeared in the distance. As they had appeared on our outward journey, rising up out of the sea, so they sunk deeper on the horizon, until nothing remained.

Hours later we steamed through the Sound of Harris and into West Loch Tarbert. The skipper sounded the horn on the boat.

We were back.

## TO TIME

Back, back
Along the road
Of time
Souls departed
Born again
A time when
Light and dark
Meant all
For food and
To survive
From one day
To the next
No clouds
Of doubt
Just rain
And time
Was still
To share and live.

This book would not be complete without saying 'Thank you' to my companions, on this, our maiden voyage to St. Kilda.

And finally, to Robert, our skipper, who turned a dream into reality.

## ABOUT THE AUTHOR

Monica Weller was born in Richmond, Surrey in 1949 and was educated at Richmond County School. She then embarked on a varied career as au-pair in Paris, floral artist at Constance Spry artificial flower studio, fashion model, toy and dolls house maker, upholsterer and footstool manufacturer, before taking up her present post as Trading Development Manager for Queen Elizabeth's Foundation for Disabled People. She  joined Bookham Camera Club and discovered her skills as a photographer, recently becoming an Associate of the Royal Photographic Society. She is a circuit judge for the Surrey Photographic Federation. Monica has two daughters and lives with her partner in Bookham, Surrey. 'Voyage to St. Kilda' is her first book.